D1199263

LIFE IN A Desert

by Kari Schuetz

BELLWETHER MEDIA · MINNEAPOLIS, MN

Note to Librarians, Teachers, and Parents:

Blastoff! Readers are carefully developed by literacy experts and combine standards-based content with developmentally appropriate text.

Level 1 provides the most support through repetition of high-frequency words, light text, predictable sentence patterns, and strong visual support.

Level 2 offers early readers a bit more challenge through varied simple sentences, increased text load, and less repetition of high-frequency words.

Level 3 advances early-fluent readers toward fluency through increased text and concept load, less reliance on visuals, longer sentences, and more literary language.

Level 4 builds reading stamina by providing more text per page, increased use of punctuation, greater variation in sentence patterns, and increasingly challenging vocabulary.

Level 5 encourages children to move from "learning to read" to "reading to learn" by providing even more text, varied writing styles, and less familiar topics.

Whichever book is right for your reader, Blastoff! Readers are the perfect books to build confidence and encourage a love of reading that will last a lifetime!

This edition first published in 2016 by Bellwether Media, Inc.

No part of this publication may be reproduced in whole or in part without written permission of the publisher. For information regarding permission, write to Bellwether Media, Inc., Attention: Permissions Department, 5357 Penn Avenue South, Minneapolis, MN 55419.

Library of Congress Cataloging-in-Publication Data

Schuetz, Kari, author.
  Life in a Desert / by Kari Schuetz.
    pages cm – (Blastoff! Readers. Biomes Alive!)
  Summary: "Simple text and full-color photography introduce beginning readers to life in a desert. Developed by literacy experts for students in kindergarten through third grade"– Provided by publisher.
  Audience: Ages 5-8.
  Audience: K to grade 3.
  Includes bibliographical references and index.
  ISBN 978-1-62617-316-3 (hardcover : alk. paper)
  1. Deserts–Juvenile literature. 2. Desert ecology–Juvenile literature. 3. Human geography–Juvenile literature. I. Title.
GF55.S45 2016
577.54–dc23

2015029918

Printed in the United States of America, North Mankato, MN.

Table of
Contents

The Desert Biome

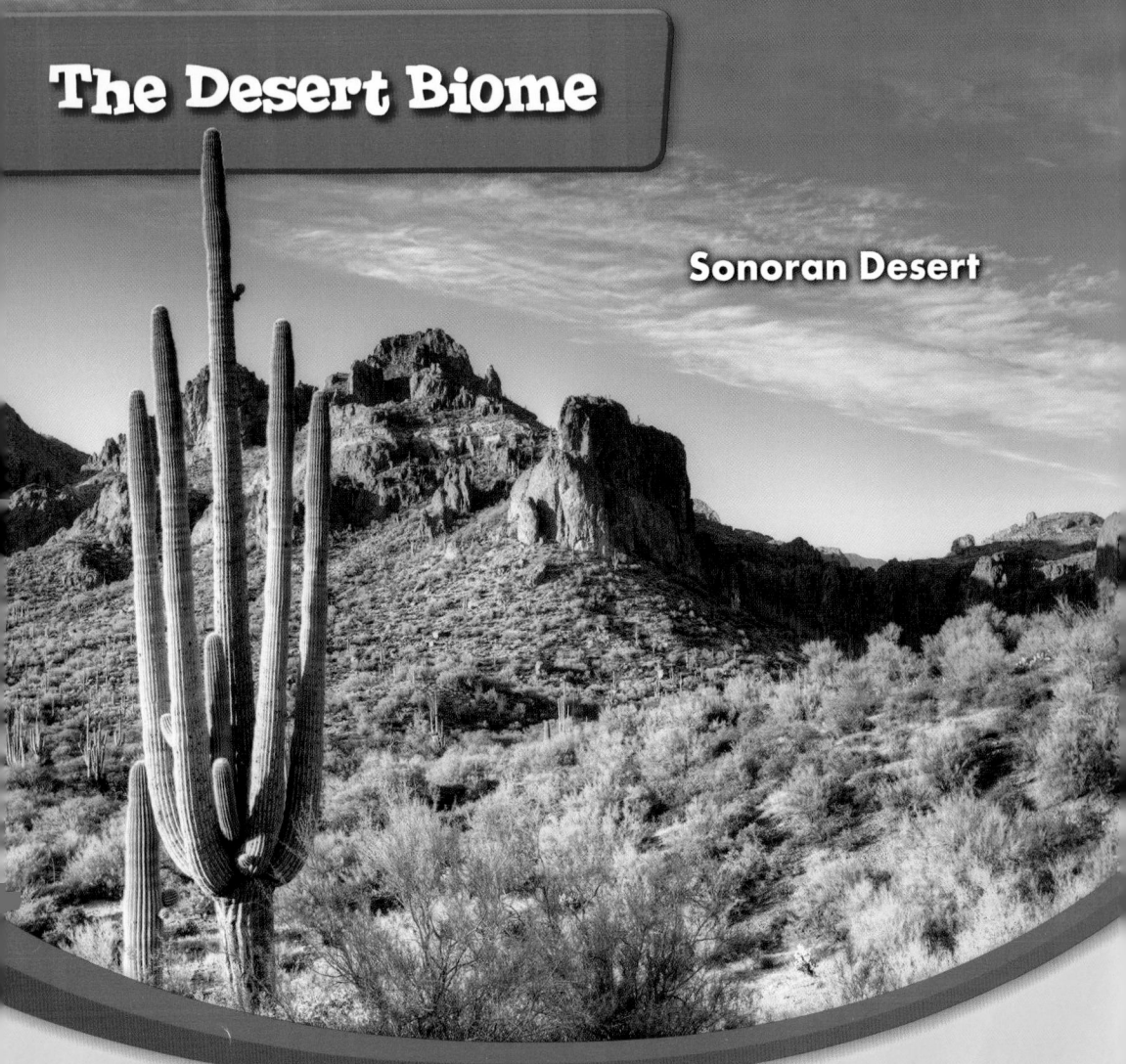

Sonoran Desert

Earth's driest **biome** is the desert. Less than 10 inches (25 centimeters) of **precipitation** falls in a desert per year.

This biome looks empty. Sand or ice and snow can cover the rocky ground.

Gobi Desert

polar deserts =

cold deserts =

hot deserts =

equator

N

W — E

S

Deserts often lie close to the **tropics**. Their location near the **equator** makes most hot.

South Pole

Cooler deserts usually lie farther north and south. The largest and coldest one is at the **South Pole**!

The Climate

Arizona Strip desert

All deserts have a dry **climate**. Any precipitation usually comes in a short burst.

Strong winds hit often. They can change the look of the land. Winds blow sand or snow into **dunes**.

dune

Temperatures in the hottest deserts go above 100 degrees Fahrenheit (38 degrees Celsius). The coldest deserts stay below **freezing** most of the time.

Antarctic Desert

Sharqiya Sands,
Oman

The change in temperature from day to night is extreme. Few clouds are present to block the sun or trap its heat.

bean caper

Desert plants have to live on little water. Their unusual leaves keep them from drying out. Many are tiny and waxy to seal in water.

Some plants have hairy leaves or **spines**. These protect the plants from the sun and even hungry animals!

grandfather cactus

The **roots** of some desert plants grow very deep. This helps them collect and hold as much water as possible.

roots

prickly pear cactus

Collected water flows to other plant parts. Those parts **swell** to store it.

fennec fox

Desert animals try to avoid extreme temperatures. **Nocturnal** creatures hide underground during the day. They come out when the sun goes down.

Other animals rest by rocks and plants. They find shade and cover from the wind.

oryx

desert
wood rat

oasis

Animals struggle to find water in
the desert. It usually comes from
plants, insects, or other foods.
Sometimes there is an **oasis**.

Some animals live on stored fat from their tail or hump. Camels can go weeks without drinking water!

dromedary camel

The Sahara Desert

Location: Africa; Algeria, Chad, Egypt, Libya, Mali, Mauritania, Morocco, Niger, Sudan, Tunisia, Western Sahara

Size: 3,300,000 square miles (8,600,000 square kilometers); largest hot desert in the world

Temperature:

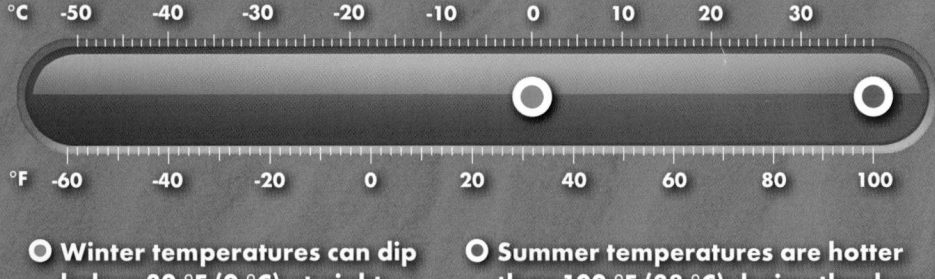

○ Winter temperatures can dip below 32 °F (0 °C) at night

○ Summer temperatures are hotter than 100 °F (38 °C) during the day

Precipitation: less than 4 inches (10 centimeters) per year in most areas

SAHARA DESERT FOOD WEB

monitor lizard

fennec fox

jerboa

horned viper

dung beetle

desert bunchgrass

Other important plants: doum palms, date palms, acacia trees, thyme trees, olive trees, oleanders, mastic trees, salt cedars, lovegrasses

Other important animals: golden jackals, dorcas, gazelles, deathstalker scorpions, ostriches, dromedary camels (no longer wild)

Glossary

biome—a nature community defined by its climate, land features, and living things

climate—the specific weather conditions for an area

dunes—hills of sand or snow created by the wind

equator—the imaginary line that divides Earth into northern and southern halves

freezing—32 degrees Fahrenheit (0 degrees Celsius); the temperature at which water freezes.

nocturnal—active at night

oasis—a desert area with water and plants

precipitation—water that falls to the earth from the sky

roots—the underground parts of a plant; roots hold a plant in place and take in water.

South Pole—Earth's southernmost point

spines—hard, sharp points

swell—to increase in size

tropics—a hot region near the equator

To Learn More

AT THE LIBRARY

Davies, Nicola. *Desert*. London, U.K.: Kingfisher, 2012.

Murphy, Julie. *Desert Animal Adaptations*. Mankato, Minn.: Capstone Press, 2012.

Royston, Angela. *Desert Food Chains*. Chicago, Ill.: Heinemann Library, 2015.

ON THE WEB

Learning more about deserts is as easy as 1, 2, 3.

1. Go to www.factsurfer.com.

2. Enter "deserts" into the search box.

3. Click the "Surf" button and you will see a list of related web sites.

With factsurfer.com, finding more information is just a click away.

Index

The images in this book are reproduced through the courtesy of: Tania Thomson, front cover (vulture left); Maria Jeffs, front cover (vulture right); Ryan M. Bolton, front cover (snake); Anton Foltin, front cover (background), p. 4; Colin Monteath/ Age Fotostock/ SuperStock, p. 5; Tom Bean/ Alamy, p. 8; Oscar Bjarnason/ Cultura Limited/ SuperStock, p. 9; Colin Harris/ era-images/ Alamy, p. 10; Matteo Colombo/ Getty Images, p. 11; Azel2101, p. 12; Paul B. Moore, p. 13; Michael Kraus, p. 14; Eutoch, p. 15; Laszlokupi, p. 16; Louise Bleakly/ Getty Images, p. 17; Animals Animals/ SuperStock, p. 18 (top); Patrick Poendl, pp. 18 (bottom), 19; somchaij, p. 20; Eric Isselee, p. 21 (monitor lizard); dangdumrong, p. 21 (fennec fox); reptiles4all, p. 21 (jerboa); efendy, p. 21 (dung beetle); N Mrtgh, p. 21 (desert bunchgrass); Ivan Kuzmin, p. 21 (horned viper).